happily grateful

Compiled by Dan Zadra with Kristel Wills
Designed by Jessica Phoenix
Created by Kobi Yamada

COMPENDIUM
INCORPORATED

live inspired.

ACKNOWLEDGEMENTS

These quotations were gathered lovingly but unscientifically over several years and/or were contributed by many friends or acquaintances. Some arrived—and survived in our files—on scraps of paper and may therefore be imperfectly worded or attributed. To the authors, contributors and original sources, our thanks, and where appropriate, our apologies. –The Editors

WITH SPECIAL THANKS TO

Jason Aldrich, Gerry Baird, Jay Baird, Neil Beaton, Josie Bissett, Laura Boro, Melissa Carlson, M.H. Clark, Tiffany Parente Connors, Jim & Alyssa Darragh & Family, Rob Estes, Pamela Farrington, Michael & Leianne Flynn & Family, Sarah Forster, Dan Harrill, Michael J. Hedge, Liz Heinlein & Family, Renee Holmes, Jennifer Hurwitz, Heidi Jones, Sheila Kamuda, Michelle Kim, Carol Anne Kennedy, June Martin, David Miller, Carin Moore & Family, Moose, Josh Oakley, Tom DesLongchamp, Steve & Janet Potter & Family, Joanna Price, Heidi & José Rodriguez, Diane Roger, Alie Satterlee, Kirsten & Garrett Sessions, Andrea Shirley, Jason Starling, Brien Thompson, Helen Tsao, Anne Whiting, Heidi Yamada & Family, Justi & Tote Yamada & Family, Bob and Val Yamada, Kaz & Kristin Yamada & Family, Tai & Joy Yamada, Anne Zadra, August & Arline Zadra, and Gus & Rosie Zadra.

CREDITS

Compiled by Dan Zadra with Kristel Wills
Designed by Jessica Phoenix
Created by Kobi Yamada

ISBN: 978-1-932319-56-9

May the joy that you give to others
be the joy that comes back to you.

"We are most alive," wrote Thornton Wilder, "when our hearts are conscious of our treasures."

This is the gift—to hear and enjoy life's music everywhere. To be more aware of what we have than what we don't have. To appreciate again and again all the wonderful things in life that money can't buy—the wind in your hair, the sun on your face; a child's laughter, a loving family, a great friend.

Truly, there is something in every day and in every season to celebrate with thanksgiving. In the end, of course, it's not what we have in our life, but who we have in our life that brings us joy.

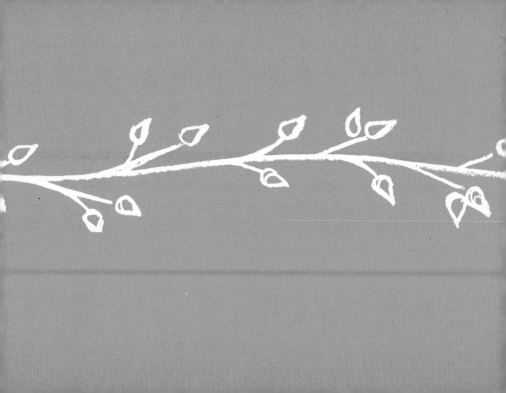

The most precious things
of life are near at hand.

JOHN BURROUGHS

All the really great things in life
are expressed in the simplest words:
friends and family; purpose and meaning;
love and work; caring and community;
appreciation and gratitude.

DAN ZADRA

My happiness derives
from knowing the people
I love are happy.

HOLLY KETCHEL

This is the gift—to have the wonderful capacity to appreciate again and again, freshly and naively, the basic goods of life, with awe, pleasure, wonder, and even ecstasy.

ABRAHAM MASLOW

Life itself is a gift.
It's a compliment just
being born: to feel, breathe,
think, play, dance, sing,
work, and make love for
this particular lifetime.

DAPHNE ROSE KINGMA

This day is a journey,
this very moment an adventure.

REBECCA PAVLENKO

Today a new sun rises
for me; everything lives,
everything is animated,
everything seems to
speak to me of my passion,
everything invites me
to cherish it.

ANNE DE LENCLOS

Stop every now and
then. Just stop and enjoy.

Take a deep breath. Relax and
take in the abundance of life.

UNKNOWN

Abundance is not something we acquire.
It is something we tune into.

WAYNE DYER

The aim of life is to live,
and to live means to be
aware, joyously, drunkenly,
divinely aware.

HENRY MILLER

We are most alive in those moments when our hearts are conscious of our treasures.

THORNTON WILDER

What is life for?
It is for you.

ABRAHAM MASLOW

The sun does not shine for a few trees and flowers, but for the wide world's joy, including yours.

HENRY WARD BEECHER

Joy seems to me a step beyond happiness. Happiness is a sort of atmosphere you can live in sometimes when you're lucky. Joy is a light that fills you with hope and faith and love.

ADELA ROGERS ST. JOHNS

Remember that feeling as a child when you woke up and the morning smiled? It's time you felt like that again.

TAJ MAHAL

Every day that we wake up is a good day. Every breath that we take is filled with hope for a better day. Every word that we speak is a chance to change what is bad into something good.

WALTER MOSLEY

The more you praise and celebrate your life, the more there is in life to celebrate.

OPRAH WINFREY

The world is grand, awfully
big and astonishingly beautiful,
frequently thrilling.

DOROTHY KILGALLEN

Not what we have, but what we

enjoy, constitutes our abundance.

JOHN PETIT-SENN

Each day comes to me with both hands full of possibilities.

HELEN KELLER

Stretch out your hand and receive the world's wide gift of joy, appreciation and beauty.

CORINNE ROOSEVELT ROBINSON

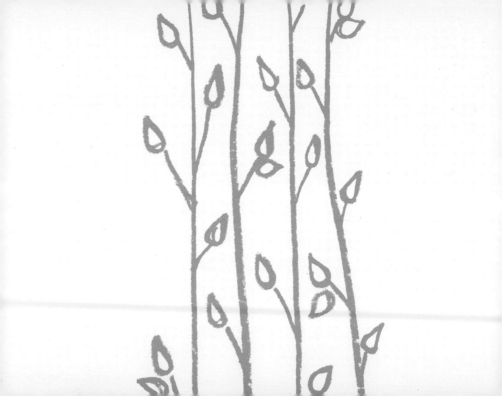

Every single day do something
that makes your heart sing.

MARCIA WIEDER

One of the sanest, surest, and most encompassing joys of life comes from being happy over the good works and good fortune of others.

ARCHIBALD RUTLEDGE

Never squander
an opportunity
to tell someone
you love or
appreciate them.

KELLY ANN ROTHAUS

Every time we remember
to say "thank you,"

we experience
heaven on earth.

SARAH BAN BREATHNACH

People love and appreciate others, not just for who they are, but for how they make us feel.

IRWIN FREEDMAN

Happiness itself is a kind of gratitude.

JOSEPH W. KRUTCH

I would maintain that thanks
are the highest form of thought;
and that gratitude is happiness
doubled by wonder.

G.K. CHESTERTON

Joy is what happens to us when we allow ourselves to recognize how good things really are.

MARIANNE WILLIAMSON

If you want to feel rich, just
count all the gifts you have
that money cannot buy.

PROVERB

Life, even in the hardest times,
is full of moments to savor.
They will not come this way
again, not in this way.

PAULA RINEHART

Each moment of the year has its own beauty...
a picture which was never seen before and
shall never be seen again.

RALPH WALDO EMERSON

Love this moment, and the energy of this moment will spread beyond all boundaries.

CORITA KENT

Look at things as though you
are seeing them either for
the first or the last time.
Then your time on earth
will be filled with glory.

BETTY SMITH

Today I live in the quiet,
joyous expectation of good.

ERNEST HOLMEN

I have a heart with room for every joy.

P.J. BAILEY

Gratitude before me and behind me.
Gratitude to the left of me and the right of me.

Gratitude above and below me.

Gratitude within and all around me.

ANGELES ARRIEN

All the great blessings of my life
are present in my thoughts today.

PHOEBE CARY

For memory has painted this
perfect day with colors that never fade,
and we find at the end of a perfect day
the soul of a friend we've made.

CARRIE JACOBS BOND